Objective
Paranormal
Investigating

Shawn Thomas

I dedicate this work to the hardworking investigators I have worked with and gotten to know over the last ten years.

CONTENTS

OTHER WORKS BY THIS AUTHOR

Redemption!
Containing the Secret Success Guide

The Reminder

And coming soon...

Nikkis

Shawn's newest inspirational novel

If you would like to contact author Shawn Thomas,
he personally responds to all e-mails sent to
shawnthomasauthor @gmail.com.

Introduction

About the author

My name is Shawn Thomas. Even though I traditionally write fiction novels with a self-help, inspirational message, I chose to write this guide to inform those who want to help people with what they believe are paranormal experiences. More so than the thrill seeking, superficial attempts so many viewers see on television every week. I began investigating when I was only 16. The only reason why I was allowed to join was because one of my friends older sisters was a member of the group and she convinced them to let me in. I began investigating in December, 2003. I have seen many people join "with the bandwagon" of television fame. So many want to get their fifteen minutes of fame. Not me, I had been investigating for nearly a year by the time "Ghost Hunters" premiered (October 6th, 2004). In fact, I have relished in the fact that I am not on, or corresponding with any production companies, past or present. It seems to me to be more of a curse than a blessing. I have been a part of multiple groups, and have founded/run a few myself, also. Television's curse has made it very difficult for groups both to stay intact and keep members simply because when people realize not everyone can be famous, they lose interest.

As part of the introduction, I'm going to go over a few of the basics that I think people should know about themselves before attempting to help others with possible paranormal experiences. I also hope to outline good sources of information to help your perspective clients, both in the introduction and throughout this guide.

Why do I want to be a paranormal investigator?

If you are first joining the field, or if you are increasing your seriousness in the field, why is an important question to ask. When I first joined, it was actually to impress my friends. For the first year I continued investigating to try to impress my friends sister (the one who got me in the first group I was a member of). I didn't even believe in ghosts when I first started. It took almost the first year before I started to believe. Contrary to what you might think, my opinion started to change after a personal experience I had far away from any paranormal investigation. After this experience, I decided that I needed to get more serious if I am ever going to find out why I experienced what I, to this day, still believe I experienced. I left the first group I was in shortly after because the two more serious members went away (they were members of the military). Two of the more experienced members, though not as serious, started a new group. In order to stay active in the field, I went along with them. I spent two years with that group. Unfortunately, it too eventually succumbed to the pressure within the field revolving around the television curse. From there, I started my own group, but no one wanted to stay in it once they discovered we weren't going to be on television. I bounced in and out of several other groups before starting what is now known as the Ludlow Paranormal Researchers.

So why do you want to investigate? It's an important question you should really be turning over in your head. Over and over. Might I suggest one piece of advice, if you are in this to try to be famous or on television or the center of attention somewhere, don't. You'll lose interest in three months or so, then probably drag down any group you join for at least a few more months before you and that group finally part ways.

From my experience, there are a few goods reasons to investigate, which I would like to share. In no way are these the only reasons. However, whatever your reason, it should be selfless. There is a lot of sacrifice. It is also a very expensive field to be in, considering no honest group charges for their services. All of your equipment and materials need to come from somewhere. My recommended reasons; To learn about the science of the field (there is a lot of it, though still in its infancy). The other reason, to help others in need.

"I've had experiences since I was a child"

That's a cute thing to say telling some campfire story with boy scouts in the woods. However, it is not something that you should promote as an investigator. (Note: if you claim to be a medium or psychic, long time experiences may help you. Although, most sensitives don't investigate scientifically). Please, accurately portray your experience, and always seek and double check information scientifically.

There is NO PROOF of ghosts in the world

Though more people believe in ghosts than don't in the world now, there is still no definitive proof that they exist. As a scientific investigator, you should always keep this in mind. All investigating, research and experiments you conduct should be attempting to find logical answers that are provable whenever possible. In this field, sometimes you can't find answers, and that's okay. Someday you might learn something to find the answer. Maybe someday we'll know that it's in fact paranormal. In the mean time, don't be afraid to say, 'I don't know'.

Have Fun

This is so much more important than I can ever accurately stress. If you are going to be a part of this field, be happy to be a part of it. If you aren't, you never get what you want out of it.

Equipment

A lot of fuss is made in many facets of the paranormal field about equipment. It seems like every season of every paranormal show they have boxes on top of boxes of new equipment. This is SO unrealistic for even the most affluent of paranormal investigators, as well as unnecessary.

I'm going to go over, what I feel, is necessary for any investigator to have whenever they are investigating (especially if they are investigating at night).

Basics

First, and most importantly, a flashlight. Day or night a flashlight can come in handy to see where you're going, or to find something in a dark area of a location. L.P.R. NEVER allows investigators to be present on any location site without a flashlight, ever.

Second, a first aid kit. I can tell you, from memory, at least six events that happened on an investigation where someone needed a first aid kit. This is without thinking, I have probably been present another six to ten times that one was necessary. I can also remember two incidents when investigators were so badly hurt they should have gone to the hospital. Please take any safety precautions you can. You may thank yourself one day.

Third, batteries, and when you think you have enough, get more. Most equipment uses batteries and you end up in situations a lot where batteries get drained faster than you expect (not of a paranormal nature).

Fourth, multi-plug units, for the equipment that can be recharged, make sure you have some place to plug it in. Extension cords won't hurt either. Anything to make sure your equipment continue working through your investigation.

Cameras

Having video cameras are important, especially those with night vision capabilities. I will recommend that 'infra-red' only or 'ultra-violet' only cameras should not be your first camera. I recommend a camera with a 'night shot' or 'night vision' capability that can also be used during the day. This will give you much more flexibility as you get started. Getting more/additional cameras will help as you go. Start simple and flexible. With the technology nowadays, your cameras should all be digital and computer compatible. This will make it a lot easier to review and store information and possible evidence.

While I'm on the subject of cameras, I want to also mention security cameras. I beg of all investigators to recognize that images captured by these cameras should NEVER be regarded as evidence. Security cameras are usually low resolution and poor quality. If you do chose to use them, please do so for gathering information like, who is where, what may be moving, outside lights coming in or other changes to your locations surroundings and conditions.

One last point about cameras I would like to make, cell phone cameras are NOT suitable pieces of equipment. Many groups that do not know any better will use their camera phones. What they do not realize is the poor quality capture all camera phones have, especially in dark conditions. Also, cell phones cause interference with other equipment, especially EMF detectors. The only exception to this plea of not using cell phones is when you are attempting to recreate a client experience using a cell phone camera.

Audio Recorders

Audio recording is still the most popular method of 'evidence' capture. This is the one area for equipment I feel an investigator can never have enough of. However, keep in mind, you still want to keep a scientific outlook on all recordings you gather. Try different recorders. Some have internal microphones, some have external ones. Having multiple microphone designs can really help you find or debunk possible evidence due to the different pickups and styles of the microphones. One prerequisite I would consider, in today's age is making sure any recorder can be directly connected to any computer or laptop. (Make sure you get a program for your computer to review it)

Electromagnetic Field Detectors (EMF Detectors)

There are many types of EMF detectors. First I am going to start by saying; Never, under any circumstance should an actual investigator ever purchase, use or trust a KII Meter. They are inconsistent at best and their readings are often manipulated by greatly non-paranormal occurrences. For example, heightened geomagnetic activity, can cause it to spike erratically.

Also, many detectors have different functions for everyday use. My recommendation is to do research on the proper way to use each detector before using it as part of an investigation. One example is the very popular Tri-field Meter. Many television groups use this piece of equipment, however they all seem to use it wrong. This meter is meant to be stationary when in use. In fact, it should be put in place before even being turned on. Moving around with this meter will make it as inconsistent as the dreaded KII.

My recommendation is one with a moving needle that focuses as much as possible in the 0-5 milligaus range. The meter I, the author, use is the 'Ghost Meter'. My reason for this is because it is simple, accurate and allows me to do what I need to while assisting my clients. It only reads in the 0-5 milligaus range, but that's all I need it to read. If readings are higher, it buries the needle and I will usually know how to approach the situation.

Thermometers/Hydrometers

It is very important to document you environment while you investigate. Keeping track of the temperature and the humidity of the location you are at can be very telling as to many personal experiences a client will call you in for. Please keep in mind, your not looking for a phantom cold spot. A small table top meter should work just fine for any objective investigator.

Don't Get Too Much

There are so many other pieces of equipment in the field being used today. Laser grids, REM pods, iphones, ovilus, ghost radars. Mel meters (EMF detectors with thermometers on them), Ghost box, thermal imaging cameras, etc. There is only one problem... You don't really need any of them. Sure its fun to try out some new gadgets out, and being as scientific as you are, I'm sure you'll try a few. Just remember, no 'paranormal research equipment' is proven to find anything that is actually paranormal. Plan your equipment budget accordingly.

Also, if you are of a mechanical inclination, don't be afraid to create your own equipment. Just make sure that you have scientific discovery in mind. As I said, ghosts are still unproven, trying to invent equipment to prove them may be impossible for the time being. So, create equipment to find more answers, not more questions.

Client Qualifying (Knowing whether or not to take a case)

Clients can be extremely difficult. There are three categories I've broken my perspective clients into. Also keep in mind, I don't take every case that comes into my hands. Qualifying the possibility of doing a thorough investigation is very important.

First, clients who the investigator has called on. This may be a public or well known location. It could also be a home that your group may have been referred to by another client. Second, clients who think that there may be activity in their property. Third, clients who are afraid of possible activity on their property. I'm going to break down and discuss each individually.

Clients You Call On

Clients you call on are clients that you are committing to conduct an investigation for just by asking in the first place. Usually, these clients are fairly difficult to interact with at first. However, if you are persistent, professional and honest, they will eventually open up to you. If their property has a great reputation you need to add extra caution in your scientific stand point and be careful not to disappoint or offend them.

Some locations may even have "haunted tours" or other attractions to entice ghost seekers to their location. Make sure anything you do doesn't affect their business. Knowing the truth is important, however, being sued for destroying someones business can devastate your life. Please be cautious.

Clients who think they may be experiencing activity

These clients are usually the easiest to deal with. They have many questions and usually few assumptions of the answers. One issue you may run into is that they will be least likely to give you all of the information you are seeking while you are qualifying the case.

Clients who are afraid of possible activity

Clients afraid of having activity in their property can be very difficult. Almost every word they say to you will be questioned inside themselves. They may even state or ask several times if they are crazy. Make sure you reassure them as much as possible, they are not. People are afraid of what they don't know or understand. Let them know they are not alone and that it is okay. It goes a long way to helping your purpose.

What You Should Be Qualifying

Everybody who investigates knows they need to know where it is, what they're investigating and who they're investigating. There are several other factors any good scientific investigator should be looking for. Before I get into detail, please know, never be afraid to ask tough questions. Sometimes people may be confused, but it is your job to be thorough. Also, keep in mind, when you ask tough questions, you should also be sympathetic. Do not be judgmental. Below are some of the harder things that L.P.R. asks when conducting a client interview. There are obviously many other related questions that can be included. Add questions as you see fit within your own cases.

First medical background can be key. Hereditary mental disorders and other developed issues can alter ones state of mind. Making them more or less susceptible to paranormal activity. One of our interview questions are as follows;

"Have any occupants ever suffered from, been diagnosed with, or tested for; Dementia, Alzheimer's, Glaucoma, Multiple Personality Disorder, Schizophrenia, Bi-polar, Manic Depression, Psychosis, PTSD, Sleep Disorders (ex. Insomnia, Sleep Paralysis), asthma, COPD (or other severe respiratory conditions)?"

Let me say there are many other disorders that can cause a person to have experiences that may be perceived as paranormal. Our reason for including only what is included is because these disorders are much more commonly found in our cases than others. Also important during the interview process is finding out if any occupants have allergies. These discoveries can lead to finding possible answers of some of their claims of activity, even before you turn on a flashlight!

One other tough question is asking occupants about any medications prescribed or otherwise they may be taking. Certain medications when mixed or taken at certain times can have an odd effect on the body and cause experiences to happen that aren't actually happening. There are many places on the internet you can go to research these side effects once you know what the medications are. I also try to learn if they have ever recreationally use illegal drugs. This is a topic you need to approach VERY sensitively. Make sure they understand you are not trying to get them into any trouble, you are just trying to help them find answers to the questions they contacted you for in the first place.

Other questions or topics discussed with clients should most likely include questions about their beliefs on what they are experiencing, and their beliefs on paranormal activity itself. Getting into their mind a little can really help you as an investigator find a good plan of attack for their concerns, or a good way out.

Also, question any theories they have already developed about their experiences. Why did they come to that conclusion? What logic was used? Did they do any research on their own?

There is always more that can be added to this part of an investigation based on how you would like to operate as an investigator. However, I personally use client, and witness interviews to determine whether or not I will take a case. Some questions I ask myself are as follows; Does this client seem to be honest or genuine? Are these claims able to be debunked or recreated? Are my findings going to be considered and appreciated by the client, even if they don't like the outcome? It's very important that the answer is yes to those three questions at a minimum. You can be as conservative or liberal as you want when deciding to take a case.

Once you've decided that a case is ready and able to be taken, the next step is research. Arguably the second most important part of investigating a case.

Research

In the L.P.R. research is broken down into three separate parts. Background, Field and Historical research. I'll go into detail on all three individually.

Background Research

Background research has a few different levels and usually consumes the most time. The first objective of someone conducting the background research is to confirm or research the client statements during the interview. For example; a client reports multiple prescription medications they are taking for various reasons. It would be the job of the researcher to find any information about any adverse side effects the body can have from any drug individually or combined. There are actual sights online where you can find this information quite easily. Other confirmations would be researching possible natural/normal explanations of the claims of activity reported. This will further help to determine a clients memory and honesty about their experiences. It will also help to develop possible ways to debunk the claim. Occasionally you may even find the answer outright (This has actually happened to me a few times!).

Field Research

Field Research is just what it sounds like. This is usually done on site. It is important to find out about nearby bodies of water, local stone content and recent changes in the surrounding nature. Sometimes, ground acidity and contents can help to find answers (ex. If the ground has high metal contents, it can effect EMF fields. Or certain fungi that could effect allergies). Also, local man made products such as wells, dams or high tension wires can assist you with finding answers for activity. Reasons for this research are quite simple. The information your looking for will help you to find possible sources for infrasound, seismic waves, EMF fields and possible molds and mildews that can effect a person enough for them to have perceived experiences. The results of this research will sometimes answer many claims of activity and will also help to design experiments for debunking other claims.

A quick note I would like to make, whenever possible, please take samples and find research to back up your findings when presenting to a client. It is very common for a client to be in complete denial that the infrasound caused by the dam overflowing behind their house could be the reason they think they see their dearly departed Aunt Peggy.

Also, part of field research is gathering weather information for the times you are on site either experimenting or investigating. We will generally keep track of the following on an hourly basis: temperature, relative humidity, barometric pressure, geomagnetic activity, solar activity, wind speed and direction, dew point. We also keep track of precipitation in previous 24 hours and during time on site (if applicable), current moon phase, passing of weather fronts in previous 24 hours and during time on site. All this information is very important because weather patterns are known to effect the human brain and its perception of its surroundings.

Historical Research

Historical research has a few different levels as well. Obviously you want to find out if anything important happened there. You also want to know if there is/was a history of domestic violence in the home. Or has there ever been a significant fire in the building (all public record). This research is key to putting together any final pieces of the story of the house. Almost a "why this house might have activity" report. Sometimes, if you feel its necessary, maybe you also conduct a background check on the client themselves (L.P.R. reserves the right to background check any client as a condition of our taking the case. We do this for our safety.). I will recommend only to do this when you feel it is completely necessary. You will rarely answer any claims of activity with this information, however, your findings may help piece together any unexplainable evidence you may find.

Good Sources of Information

Obviously, it is easy to go on the internet and look up a lot of information to help your investigation. Make sure you fact check though whenever you do use the internet, it won't always be correct. However, there are a few places you should know about for information you may not be able to find online. Examples; Town offices for background or historical research. This would include, town assessor, town clerk, police or fire department. Town historians can be good sources of information, however be careful, they can sometimes be closed minded and cause you more headaches than they relieve. Local libraries can sometimes hold information on a property. The older the property is, usually the easier it is to find information in libraries. Also, tracking deeds for ownership and related properties (which sometimes can hold their own histories and further your research) at the local Registry of Deeds/ Deed Annex can be extremely helpful (personally, looking through the annex books is one of my favorite things to do while conducting research).

When you and your group is completed with its research, make sure you organize and keep as much research as you can, at a bare minimum, anything related to any findings you have made (paranormal or not).

Experimentation/Debunking

This section is the hardest to write about, yet in the eyes of most clients, will be the most telling of what may be happening. Even though most clients are eagerly awaiting an all night "ghost hunt" complete with night vision cameras and funky gear. When you thoroughly explain this entire investigation process to a client, they tend to key in on this particular date on your investigation calendar.

I recommend holding a meeting following all of the interviews and research being completed. Go over all the claims of activity, then review the research. Eliminate any claims of activity the research you conducted justifiably answered. Then look at the remaining claims. Finally, develop any experiments you can realistically complete to attempt to answer the remaining claims.

Some simple tests are as follows; Mold cultures, are normally good attempting to debunk odors. However, sometimes, molds and mildews with greater side effects can be found. Some can cause brain damage, respiratory issues or even death. Conducting this simple test can not only answer many claims, it may also save someone's life.

Make sure you examine any possible way to test if possible 'sightings' could be the result of pareidolia. Basically, pareidolia is your brain creating a false image in a foreign object of similar shape (ex. Your brain is trained to make faces out of anything possible to recognize friendliness or danger based on shape)

Current tests on electrical sources throughout the home (especially lights) can help with claims of electrical issues.

Rolling ball/water droplet testing can help determine if floors are slightly off causing feelings of vertigo or dizziness which could lead to paranoia and sometimes hallucinations, among other issues. This test is basically using a ball or small amount of water on the floor and seeing if and in what way it moves (balls are better for this test). In most homes, the ball will move. What you are looking for is sudden, hastening or erratic movement.

There are many different ways to test claims of activity, sometimes just playing with a flashlight in an area across the room or on reflective surfaces. Possibly playing with camera functions determining if a camera malfunctions ruined a 'family' photo.

Open multiple doors to test changing pressure in the location or other doors moving without apparent contact. (A lot of fun to show clients if it works in their home)

When conducting experiments, I beg of you, please do not spend time doing one of the phony 'contact tests'. These tests are when an investigator takes a KII meter or a flashlight, and tries to entice responses from possible "spirits". These tests are in no way scientific, objective or even accurate. There are much better ways to investigate then this.

Though this is a very short section, take it very seriously. Make sure you develop and plan your experiments thoroughly. Your client will key in on the results. Preparing and conducting these experiments will usually answer the last of the clients claims. Although sometimes, a few claims will remain. Just a few things left you can't explain. That's when we finally get to the "night investigation".

A side note; during the experimentation session on location, and during any time you are on a clients property, as many recorders and cameras should be rolling as realistic and convenient as possible. You never know when something in your surroundings can happen right under your nose without you noticing. This can both help you to answer claims, or even help you find possible evidence supporting your clients claims. One never knows. However, a simple cardinal rule, the more information you gather, the better off you are.

Night Investigation

Please, don't call this "dead time" or "witching hour" or anything foolish like that. Also, don't restrict yourself to only a few hours in the early morning. For most of us who sleep at night when we aren't investigating, this is the worst thing you can do. As your body gets increasingly tired, it begins to process things differently and take shortcuts in order to keep your brain, heart and lungs functioning, as well as keep you able to care for yourself (this is a reaction in your brain from the area programmed with all the evolutionary 'survival of the fittest' information). One quick example, a person who has been awake for sixteen consecutive hours functions with the same brain activity (time and accuracy) as someone who had consumed two alcoholic drinks together after being awake only eight hours. The downside to all this is that it makes you more susceptible to have a personal experience, and less likely for you to be able to accurately investigate it. I normally prefer the

L.P.R. to do its night investigations from seven or eight in the evening until one or two in the morning. Sometimes I'll also have an investigation end earlier if I believe enough has been done. Rarely do I recommend to a client to investigate later than that. One exception is if a high amount of activity occurs only during those hours and I am not able to debunk it in any other way.

Before a night investigation, a brief meeting is held to organize the jobs of every member and schedule for the night. Unlike what you see on television I do not recommend investigating in groups of two (I will explain momentarily). Furthermore no one should EVER investigate by themselves. There are so many problems you can run into by yourself, liability, injury, credibility. It doesn't matter if you have a ghost tap dancing on camera, without corroboration and backed up evidence, no one will ever believe it (skeptics won't anyway).

I always recommend teams investigate in groups of three or four depending on the size of the location. However, three works the best. My reason two is not a good option is because there are so many things that can be left out, and it is much easier for two to fake an experience then three, simply because of the amount of equipment that would be around. The way my groups generally operate is one person is appointed "cameraman". His job is only to record the other investigators and relay any personal experiences. He may also be the one holding notes on things that the group may need to cover during that period of the night/investigation. The direction is for the other two investigators to stay relatively close to each other (with limited exceptions) to make it easier for the "cameraman" to document them. The whole idea is to be as reputable and professional as possible, as well finding possible answers as to why you are in that clients home.

Obviously, recording as much information as possible is key. There is not ever a single second that we are on site without a camera rolling. Sometimes, members of our group will begin filming as we pull into the clients driveway/property.

Below are a few basic rules that are actual L.P.R. investigating procedures. There are many more, and you should also develop your own to make sure your group operates the way you want.

"Self investigation is strictly prohibited. The L.P.R. defines Self Investigation as; the intentional act of an investigator to attempt to collect evidence without the knowledge or corroboration of, or giving knowledge to a second or subsequent investigator. During indoor investigations, all investigators in a group must be in the same room unless the entire group is moving to another room. During an outdoor investigation, the required space (with limited exception) is 20 feet."

"It is extremely important that investigators are extremely careful when and how they divulge personal experiences during an investigation. There must be a corroborating experience for it to be considered possibly paranormal. When an investigator feels they may have had a personal experience, they must pause and question other investigators present if they just saw/felt/heard something. If the second (or subsequent) investigator also had an experience, they will need to question the original investigator of their experience. If the experiences are the same or similar, it is expected the investigator's attempt to debunk the experience. If it is not the same, or if no other investigator had an experience, the investigation should continue normally. Integrity is extremely important. Any one found to be intentionally manufacturing evidence will be asked to leave the investigation."

"During an EVP session, limiting the amount of noise is key to capturing possible EVP's. Preferably, all investigators should be seated in a close area NOT MOVING during questions. It is expected that after a question is asked, a minimum of 20 seconds elapse (30 seconds preferred) before another question is asked. Personal experiences are a worthy exception to violate silence and should be reported to others present immediately. Also, recorders must be placed down on a solid surface out of the investigator's hand's to prevent contamination of the recording."

As you can see from these three basic principles of investigation within the group, it is very important to operate from an objective standpoint and do whatever possible not to contaminate possible evidence. One other procedure not mentioned yet is tagging. Tagging is audibly noting any possible contaminants you are aware of at the time of recording. This can help immensely during review in separating real evidence from contaminated evidence. One training exercise I like to run with my new members is to have them go to a public park during the day and for one hour, just sit and listen. Their instruction is to tag every sound they notice, especially the foreign sounds that only should only happen once or twice. Then, they are to listen to the audio to see what they have missed. It is amazing how much any investigator will miss, especially the first few times. Try it with your group.

Proper and Thorough Review

This is another section that will not be very long, but can be very important. Let me first mention that review of any recordings you take should be done throughout the investigation. I recommend completing the review of all recordings made before a night investigation, before actually conducting the night investigation. This can help to ease or at least organize a night investigation.

Audio Review

When reviewing audio, I recommend being in a quiet area. Using noise canceling or noise reducing headphones are best. Keep a detailed log of every possible instance on the recording that can help the investigation. Learning how to use an audio system on your computer will help immensely. Also, saving small cuts of your files can help you in determining possible evidence for the location. Personally I use Audacity for audio review, however, a lot of other investigators I know use Adobe Audition and they seem to be very satisfied. Either is a great choice. Others exist, however, I have not worked with them, and do not feel comfortable promoting any systems I have not used myself.

EVP Grading

One thing that I have come across in my time, is that people tend to grade EVP's. The first thing I would like to say is that there is NO official grading scale for EVP. However, the pressures of this field has forced the groups I have run to adopt a 'grading' scale. Let me repeat, this is NOT an official scale. This however, does provide a quality scale that I can easily explain to clients if needed. My classifications are Class A, Class B, Class U. Each qualification is determined on an EVP grading scale I have developed (again NOT an official scale) and is detailed below. As you could probably guess, my class A is going to be high quality EVP. To be considered Class A it MUST have 10 out of a possible 10 points. In over 200 investigations I believe I have recorded less than five class A. Class B scores in the 7-9 point range. However, it MUST be multiple syllables. One syllable 'words' can too easily be something organic happening and the sound being changed by the acoustics of its surroundings, or by the device capturing it. Class U, or an Unusable EVP, will score 4-6 points (7 points if one syllable). I will usually throw those out of consideration as possible 'evidence'. It is rarely more than a blip in my overall report. I will almost never present Class U to a client unless a client is demanding to hear it. Any scores of 3 points or less is dismissed as non-evidence completely. Usually I will only save clips scoring 1-3 points to use in group 'trainings'. We use them to attempt to train our ears, brains and logical thinking to attempt to debunk, helping us on future cases.

EVP Scale

1. Audio clear (zero-minimal interference): one point

2. No investigator's talking (five seconds before or after): one point

3. Speech audible: one point

4. Multiple syllable: one point

5. Pitch does not match present investigators (or guests): one point

6. Audio wavelength different than other investigators normal speech: one point

7. No tagged exotic sounds in previous or following 30 seconds: one point

8. Relevant response to question or location: one point

9. Easily recognized by first time listeners without amplification or cleaning: two points

Video Review

When reviewing Video, I still recommend uploading it to your computer and using noise canceling headphones. However, I also recommend reviewing video in a dark room in order to focus your attention on the video playing in front of you (another fascinating fact about your brain is that your mind is attracted to focus on light very similar to most insects). Again, save any clips of video necessary and keep a complete log of possible findings and evidence.

When you've finished, prepare a final report and move on to the next section. Final reports should contain at a minimum, the following; discoveries made through research (print outs whenever possible), results of all tests/experiments, record of any 'current conditions' (like the weather, or contamination's) while on site, list of 'material gathered' (hours of recordings, audio and video), detail of possible evidence recovered (both stats of possible evidence and detail of the nature of possible evidence), final opinion and conclusions based on discoveries, and finally, recommended followup schedule.

Case Reveal/Client Relations

How you close a case is equally important to how you start one. It is the last impression they have as you. First impressions will tend to be personal, last impressions tend to be professional driven. It is extremely important to leave your clients with a good feeling.

First, the final report I mentioned. Whether you conduct a night investigation or not, there are many sources of research and discovery over the course of each case. It is extremely important to organize everything into a report that both answers the clients questions/concerns, and also makes them feel as comfortable as you possibly can make them. Make sure you print it out and give them a copy. It will give them reassurance that they can trust your findings.

Next, make a followup schedule with the client (try to already have one recommended in your report). This lets them know you aren't just going to forget about them. This also helps them to feel reassured that they can trust your opinions and findings. What I have always attempted to do was to at least call a client every three months for the first year after closing the investigation. Sometimes I will continue contact on a semi-regular basis even after that. A ten minute phone call just to see how things are going goes a very long way. It also helps to build trust if they continue to have issues in their home. It is always a great feeling to know they are happy to hear from you.

Another important step is to ensure their privacy. Even though you may retain the right (as L.P.R. does) to use any recorded image as you see fit, make sure you take your clients wishes about privacy into consideration. Don't be afraid to talk to them about it, either. Just make sure you keep any promise you make to them.

Encourage them to spread the word about your group, they may know other people going through the same thing. They may also know someone interested in getting into the field as well. They may just know someone really interested in your work and they can really spread the word about your group. One thing I know for certain, word of mouth can be your most powerful asset in this field.

Conclusion

So what do you think? Do you still want to be a paranormal investigator? I truly hope I have helped each and every reader of this short work. Please refer back to it as often as you need to, especially if you are first becoming an investigator. Also, please refer to the definitions page following this conclusion for more information on terms, phrases and words used in the field. Also, please keep in mind I am writing this as a person who began investigating ten years before the completion of this guide. I may update it in the future, I may even write a completely knew one as time moves forward. Even after ten years and 200 investigations, I am still learning every time I take on a case. I hope you will too.

Good luck to all.

Definitions

Let me first congratulate you on making it this far! Many readers will not take the time to read the definitions, even though in this field, you should. I will first start by saying this section can never be complete! However, I believe that the definitions contained here will both give you a solid foundation of information, and an avenue to start with in further research and hopefully self-education. Never pass on the chance to learn more while you are still active within the field. Also, you may notice some of the more basic or common terms in the field are not in this list. This is because I wanted to words of this list to be ones that you do not see often. I want you to use your time to learn something truly new to you.

Anemometer: A meteorological device that detects wind and measures its velocity.

Angel: A supernatural being that is believed to exist on the level between God and human kind.

Anomaly: noun, something that deviates from what is normal , expected or standard.

Apophenia: The experience of seeing meaningful patterns or connections in random or meaningless data. (see pareidolia)

Apparition: noun, A ghost or ghostlike image of a person.

Aura: A natural electromagnetic field that surrounds the body. Believed to possibly be ones soul or a metaphysical teller of one's emotional state.

Ball Lightning: A rare form of lightning in the shape of a glowing ball (usually red), can last several seconds to several minutes. Thought to consist of ionized gas.

Baseline Readings: The base or standard reading of an area or location. Measurements may be used either to find or refute possible paranormal activity.

Debunk: the act of finding as answer to a claim of possible paranormal activity.

Demon: A believed evil spirit.

Electromagnetic Field (EMF): noun, A field of force that contains both electric and magnetic components, resulting from the motion of an electric charge and containing a definite amount of electromagnetic energy.

Electronic Voice Phenomena (EVP): Sounds found on electronic recordings which resemble speech, but are reportedly not the result of intentional recording or rendering. EVP are commonly found in recordings with static, stray radio transmissions and background noise. Recordings of EVP are often produced by increasing the gain (i.e. sensitivity) of the recording equipment.

Ghost: noun, An apparition of a dead person that is believed to appear or become manifest to the living, typically as a nebulous image. Also known as a wraith, specter, phantom, spirit, presence, etc.

Hallucination: A false or distorted perception of objects or events with a full belief in their reality.

Hydrometer: An instrument of measurement used to read the relative humidity levels of its focus item or area.

Hypnagogic State: The transitional state of consciousness experienced while falling asleep.

Sometimes characterized by vivid hallucinations or imagery.

Hypnopompic State: The transitional state of consciousness experienced while awakening. Sometimes characterized by vivid hallucinations or imagery.

Infrared light: electromagnetic radiation with wavelengths longer than visible light but shorter than radio waves.

Infrasound: noun, Sound waved with frequencies below the lower limit of human audibility.

Intelligent Haunting: A label given to a haunt or ghost which is believed to be able to respond to real time and/or request.

Manifestation: an event, action or object that clearly shows or embodies something.

Metaphysics: A field of study dedicated to the nature of reality.

Milligaus: A unit of measurement for low level electromagnetic fields (mGs).

Orb: A nonsensical image (usually in spherical shape) that is often mistaken for a paranormal spirit. Generally, orbs are dust, reflections, water particles, or other items out of position for the camera to focus and clear their image.

Pareidolia: A psychological phenomenon involving a vague or random stimulus being perceived as significant, a form of apophenia.

Phenomenon: A term used to collectively describe anything that cannot be explained in scientific terms.

Radiation: the emission of energy as electromagnetic waves or as subatomic particles.

Residual Haunting: Believed to be an energy imprint. Energy absorbed by inanimate objects is sometimes released in the form of a physical manifestation.

Seismic Wave (causing vibrations): noun, An elastic wave in the earth produced by an earthquake or other means.

Sleep paralysis: An occurrence when an individual, either falling asleep or waking up, temporarily experiences the inability to move. Linked with disorders such as; narcolepsy, migraines, anxiety disorders and obstructive sleep apnea. Also common among those living in isolation. Note: approximately 36% of US population between ages of 25 and 44 experience phenomena at least once.

Thermometer: An instrument of measurement used

to read the temperature of its applied test object/area.

Ultraviolet light: radiation lying in the ultraviolet range. Wavelengths shorter than light, but longer than X-rays.

White Noise: noise containing many frequencies of equal intensity.

ABOUT THE AUTHOR

Shawn Thomas is an author of primarily fiction novels. He attempts to include a motivational/inspirational message to the reader with a message to help them find success in their life everyday. Shawn is also a decorated salesperson who has applied his trade to several different fields.